BEST OF
MOROCCO

Consultant Editor:
Valerie Ferguson

Contents

Introduction

The food of Morocco, some of the world's most fragrant and flavourful, is probably the least known and appreciated. Looking one way to the Mediterranean and the other to Africa, the country has been subject to a huge range of influences over the centuries, through trade as well as invasion. Today Moroccan cooking reflects the influence of the Berbers, Arabs, Bedouins, Spanish and French. Couscous and chick-peas, cinnamon and saffron, lemon and coriander, garlic and olives, dates and almonds – these are just a few of the varied ingredients used in this wonderfully diverse cuisine.

The national dish is couscous, which is of Berber origin. Also here are substantial soups, mouth-watering roasts, tempting tagines (a type of thick stew) and unusual vegetable dishes. Morocco's long coastline ensures tantalizing fish and seafood recipes, often using the classic marinade of *charmoula*, such as Sea Bream with Artichokes & Courgettes. Desserts include the intriguingly named Gazelles' Horns and there is a recipe for Moroccan bread, an essential accompaniment to savoury dishes.

Open this book and unveil the mystique of Moroccan cuisine.

Ingredients

If you are planning to cook Moroccan food, you will find that certain essential ingredients are called for again and again: they are the essence of the flavour of Morocco.

Fish & Seafood: Morocco boasts thousands of wonderful fish recipes as each region tends to have its own traditional dishes. Large fish, like sea bass and sea bream, are cooked whole, either stuffed or baked with vegetables. Fish is also often marinated in a combination of herbs and spices called *charmoula*.

Fruit: Moroccan markets are brimming with fabulous fresh fruit. Lemons, figs, apricots and, of course, dates are used in both sweet and savoury dishes. They are often used in their dried form, especially apricots.

Herbs: Coriander and garlic are essential herbs in Moroccan cookery, adding a wonderful pungency. Flat leaf parsley, which has a mild, fragrant flavour, is also used. Mint is very popular in salads and no Moroccan meal would be complete without refreshing mint tea.

Meat & Poultry: Lamb is the most popular red meat, featuring in tagines and simple but succulent roasts. Chicken, too, is widely enjoyed. Meat and poultry are usually cooked with spices and herbs to enhance their flavour.

Clockwise from the top: Cumin seeds, saffron threads, cayenne pepper, ground turmeric, cinnamon sticks, ground cinnamon, paprika, black peppercorns, ground cumin and ground ginger (centre).

Nuts: The most widely used nuts in Moroccan cuisine are almonds and pine nuts, which are found in both savoury and sweet dishes, and cashews.

Pulses & Grains: Chick-peas and dried broad beans are popular for dips, stews and soups. Couscous, which consists of tiny pellets of grain, is the national dish of Morocco. It is steamed and served warm with tagines, or allowed to cool and used as the basis for delicious salads. Bulgur wheat is also enjoyed.

Spices: Cinnamon is widely used in soups and tagines and mixed with sugar to dust over fried dessert pastries. Cumin is popular in fish and poultry dishes. Saffron is used in small amounts to add colour and a subtle aroma.

Clockwise from the top: Blanched, whole, flaked and shelled almonds, dried chick-peas, couscous and ground almonds (centre).

Turmeric is enjoyed for its characteristic pungency. Ground ginger, which adds a more mellow flavour than the fresh root, is the preferred choice of Moroccan cooks. Paprika is an essential element in *charmoula*. Cayenne is enjoyed in southern Morocco where food is more highly spiced.

Vegetables: Morocco grows an abundance of fresh vegetables, such as tomatoes, sweet peppers, olives, courgettes, broad beans, artichokes and aubergines. They feature in tagines and couscous dishes as well as in side dishes and salads.

Techniques

Stoning Olives

Pre-stoned olives lack the flavour and variety of whole ones, so stone them yourself if you can.

1 To remove the stone from an olive put the olive in the stoner, pointed end uppermost.

2 Squeeze the handles of the stoner together to extract the stone. Using a stoner is the easiest way to remove the stone from an olive, but you can also use a sharp knife.

Preparing Garlic

Don't worry if you don't have a garlic press: try this method, which gives wonderfully juicy results.

1 Break off the clove of garlic, place the flat side of a large knife on top and strike with your fist. Remove all the papery outer skin. Begin by finely chopping the clove.

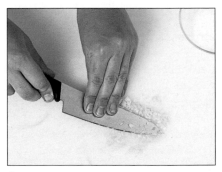

2 Sprinkle over a little table salt and, using the flat side of a large knife blade, work the salt into the garlic, until the clove softens and releases its juices. Use as required.

Chopping Herbs

Chop herbs just before you use them: the flavour will then be at its best.

1 Remove the leaves and place them on a clean, dry board. Use a large, sharp cook's knife (if you use a blunt knife you will bruise the herbs rather than chopping them) and chop them until as coarse or as fine as needed.

2 Alternatively, use a herb chopper, also called a mezzaluna, which is a very useful tool for finely chopping herbs or vegetables. Use a see-saw motion for best results.

Preserving Lemons

1 Quarter 5 lemons lengthways, to within 1 cm/½ in of the base. Sprinkle the flesh with salt and reshape the lemons.

2 Place 30 ml/2 tbsp salt in a sterilized preserving jar and press in the lemons so that they release their juice, salting between the layers. Cover completely with lemon juice. Leave for 20–30 days, shaking the jar every other day.

3 When ready to use, remove as many lemons as required and rinse under running water. Scoop out and discard the pulp. Chop the skin finely or coarsely as required. Preserved lemons should keep for up to a year.

Grinding Spices

The best flavour will be obtained if you start off with whole spices and crush them as and when needed. Crush whole spices in a coffee grinder or spice mill.

Marinated Olives

Olives absorb the flavours of these two tangy and contrasting marinades to stimulate the taste buds.

Serves 6–8

INGREDIENTS
225 g/8 oz/1⅓ cups green or tan olives
   (unpitted) for each marinade

FOR THE MOROCCAN MARINADE
45 ml/3 tbsp chopped fresh coriander
45 ml/3 tbsp chopped fresh flat leaf parsley
1 garlic clove, finely chopped
good pinch of cayenne pepper
good pinch of ground cumin
30–45 ml/2–3 tbsp olive oil
30–45 ml/2–3 tbsp lemon juice

FOR THE SPICY HERB MARINADE
60 ml/4 tbsp chopped fresh coriander
60 ml/4 tbsp chopped fresh flat leaf parsley
1 garlic clove, finely chopped
5 ml/1 tsp grated fresh root ginger
1 red chilli, seeded and finely sliced
¼ preserved lemon, cut into thin strips

1 Crack the olives to break the flesh but not the stone. Leave in cold water overnight. Drain and divide between two jars.

2 Blend the ingredients for each marinade and stir into the two jars. Store in the fridge for at least 1 week, shaking the jars occasionally.

Byesar

In Morocco this purée of dried broad beans is scooped up with bread which is first dipped in a fiery combination of spices.

Serves 4–6

INGREDIENTS
115 g/4 oz dried broad beans, soaked
2 garlic cloves, peeled
5 ml/1 tsp cumin seeds
about 60 ml/4 tbsp olive oil
salt
fresh mint sprigs, to garnish
extra cumin seeds, cayenne pepper and
   bread, to serve

1 Put the broad beans in a saucepan with the whole garlic cloves and the cumin seeds and add enough water just to cover. Bring to the boil, then reduce the heat and simmer until the broad beans are tender.

2 Drain, reserving the cooking liquid. Cool the beans and slip off the outer skin of each one.

3 Purée the beans in a blender or food processor, adding sufficient olive oil and reserved cooking liquid to give a smooth, soft dip. Season to taste with plenty of salt. Garnish with sprigs of mint and serve with bread, extra cumin seeds and cayenne pepper for dipping.

Right: Marinated Olives (top); Byesar

Sizzling Prawns

For a really tasty starter, fry prawns in a blend of Moroccan spices. It couldn't be simpler.

Serves 4

INGREDIENTS
450 g/1 lb raw king prawns in their shell
30 ml/2 tbsp olive oil
25–40 g/1–1½ oz/2–3 tbsp butter
2 garlic cloves, crushed
5 ml/1 tsp ground cumin
2.5 ml/½ tsp ground ginger
10 ml/2 tsp paprika
1.5 ml/¼ tsp cayenne pepper
lemon wedges and fresh coriander sprigs,
    to garnish

1 Keeping one prawn whole, to use as a garnish, pull the heads off the rest and then peel away the shells, legs and tails. Using a sharp knife, cut along the back of each prawn and pull away and discard the dark thread.

2 Heat the olive oil and butter and fry the garlic for about 30 seconds. Add the ground spices. Cook and stir for a few seconds, then add the prawns. Cook for 2–3 minutes over a high heat, until they turn pink, stirring frequently.

3 Serve the prawns with the spicy butter poured over and garnished with lemon wedges and coriander.

Grilled Keftas

It's important to process this dish an hour before cooking to allow the flavours to develop.

Makes 12–14

INGREDIENTS
675 g/1½ lb lamb, roughly chopped
1 onion, quartered
3–4 fresh parsley sprigs
2–3 fresh coriander sprigs
1–2 fresh mint sprigs
2.5 ml/½ tsp ground cumin
2.5 ml/½ tsp ground mixed spice
5 ml/1 tsp paprika
salt and freshly ground black pepper

FOR THE MINT DRESSING
30 ml/2 tbsp finely chopped fresh mint
90 ml/6 tbsp plain yogurt

1 Process the lamb in a food processor until smooth. Remove and process the onion and herbs until finely chopped. Add the lamb, spices and seasoning and process until very smooth. Chill for about 1 hour.

2 To make the dressing, blend the mint with the yogurt and chill. Mould the meat into sausages and skewer with kebab sticks. Grill for 5–6 minutes, turning once. Serve with the dressing.

Right: Sizzling Prawns (top);
Grilled Keftas

Meat Briouates

The Moroccans, who enjoy the taste of sweet and savoury together, traditionally sprinkle these little pastries with ground cinnamon and sugar.

Makes about 24

INGREDIENTS
175 g/6 oz filo pastry
40 g/1½ oz/3 tbsp butter, melted
sunflower oil, for frying
fresh flat leaf parsley, to garnish
ground cinnamon and icing sugar,
    to serve (optional)

FOR THE MEAT FILLING
1 onion, finely chopped
1 small bunch fresh
    coriander, chopped
1 small bunch fresh parsley, chopped
30 ml/2 tbsp sunflower oil
375 g/13 oz lean minced beef
    or lamb
2.5 ml/½ tsp paprika
5 ml/1 tsp ground coriander
good pinch of ground ginger
2 eggs, beaten

1 To make the filling, fry the onion and herbs in the oil for about 4 minutes, until the onion is soft. Add the meat and cook for about 5 minutes, stirring frequently, until the meat is evenly browned.

2 Drain away any excess fat, stir in the spices and cook for 1 minute. Remove from the heat and stir in the beaten eggs until they begin to set. Place the mixture to one side.

3 Cut a sheet of filo pastry into 9 cm/3½ in strips. Brush one strip with melted butter, then place a heaped teaspoon of the meat filling 1 cm/½ in from the end.

4 Fold one corner of the pastry over the filling to make a triangular shape. Fold the "triangle" over itself and then continue to fold, keeping the triangle shape, until you reach the end of the strip. Continue in this way until all the pastry and mixture have been used up.

5 Fry the *briouates* in batches in about 1 cm/½ in sunflower oil for 2–3 minutes until they are golden, turning once during frying. Drain the *briouates* and serve garnished with fresh flat leaf parsley and sprinkled with ground cinnamon and icing sugar, if liked.

Chick-pea & Parsley Soup

A substantial soup that benefits from the fresh, lightening flavours of parsley and lemon.

Serves 6

INGREDIENTS
225 g/8 oz/1⅓ cups chick-peas,
   soaked overnight
1 small onion
1 bunch fresh parsley (about 40 g/1½ oz)
30 ml/2 tbsp olive and sunflower oil, mixed
1.2 litres/2 pints/5 cups chicken stock
juice of ½ lemon
salt and freshly ground black pepper
lemon wedges and finely pared strips of rind,
   to garnish
Moroccan bread, to serve

1 Drain and rinse the chick-peas then cook them in boiling water for 1–1½ hours, until tender. Drain and peel (see Cook's Tip).

2 Process the onion and parsley in a food processor until finely chopped. Heat the oils and fry the mixture for about 4 minutes over a low heat, until slightly softened.

3 Add the chick-peas, cook gently for 1–2 minutes and add the stock. Season well. Bring to the boil, cover and simmer for 20 minutes, until the chick-peas are very tender.

4 Allow the soup to cool a little and then part-purée in a food processor, or by mashing the chick-peas fairly roughly with a fork, so that the soup is thick but still quite crunchy.

5 Transfer the soup to a clean pan, add the lemon juice and adjust the seasoning if necessary. Heat gently, then serve garnished with lemon wedges and finely pared rind, and accompanied by Moroccan bread.

COOK'S TIP: Chick-peas, especially canned ones, blend better in soups and other dishes if the skin is rubbed away with your fingers. This is time-consuming but well worth the effort.

Moroccan Vegetable Soup

Creamy parsnip and pumpkin give this soup a wonderfully rich texture.

Serves 4

INGREDIENTS
15 ml/1 tbsp olive or sunflower oil
15 g/½ oz/1 tbsp butter
1 onion, chopped
225 g/8 oz carrots, chopped
225 g/8 oz parsnips, chopped
225 g/8 oz pumpkin
about 900 ml/1½ pints/3¾ cups vegetable or
   chicken stock
lemon juice, to taste
salt and freshly ground black pepper

FOR THE GARNISH
7.5 ml/1½ tsp olive oil
½ garlic clove, finely chopped
45 ml/3 tbsp chopped fresh parsley and
   coriander, mixed
good pinch of paprika

2 Cut the pumpkin into chunks, discarding the skin and pith, and stir into the pan. Cover and cook for a further 5 minutes, then add the stock and seasoning and slowly bring to the boil. Cover and leave to simmer very gently for 35–40 minutes, until the vegetables are tender.

3 Allow the soup to cool slightly, then purée in a food processor or blender until smooth, adding a little extra stock if the soup is too thick. Pour into a clean saucepan, and reheat gently.

4 To make the garnish, heat the oil in a small pan and gently fry the garlic and herbs for 1–2 minutes. Add the paprika and stir well.

1 Heat the oil and butter in a large pan and fry the onion for about 3 minutes, until soft. Add the carrots and parsnips, stir well, cover and cook over a gentle heat for 5 minutes.

5 Adjust the seasoning of the soup and stir in lemon juice to taste. Pour into soup bowls and spoon a little garnish on top, which should then be carefully swirled into the soup.

Chicken Soup with Vermicelli

In Morocco, the cook would use a whole chicken for this nourishing soup. Here is a slightly simplified version, using chicken portions.

Serves 4–6

INGREDIENTS
30 ml/2 tbsp sunflower oil
15 g/½ oz/1 tbsp butter
1 onion, chopped
2 chicken legs or breasts, halved or quartered
flour, for dusting
2 carrots, cut into 4 cm/1½ in pieces
1 parsnip, cut into 4 cm/1½ in pieces
1.5 litres/2½ pints/6¼ cups chicken stock
1 cinnamon stick
good pinch of paprika
pinch of saffron
2 egg yolks
juice of ½ lemon
30 ml/2 tbsp chopped fresh coriander
30 ml/2 tbsp chopped fresh parsley
150 g/5 oz vermicelli
salt and freshly ground black pepper
Moroccan bread, to serve

1 Heat the oil and butter and fry the onion for 3–4 minutes, until softened. Dust the chicken pieces in seasoned flour and fry until browned.

2 Transfer the chicken to a plate and add the carrots and parsnip to the pan. Cook gently for 3–4 minutes, then return the chicken to the pan. Add the stock, cinnamon stick, paprika and seasoning. Bring to the boil, cover and simmer for 1 hour, until the vegetables are tender.

3 Meanwhile, blend the saffron in 30 ml/2 tbsp boiling water. Beat the egg yolks with the lemon juice in a separate bowl and add the chopped fresh coriander and parsley. When the saffron water has cooled, stir into the egg and lemon mixture.

4 When the vegetables are tender, transfer the chicken portions to a plate. Skin the chicken and, if liked, bone and chop into bite-size pieces. Spoon away any excess fat from the soup, then increase the heat, add the vermicelli and cook for 5–6 minutes, until the vermicelli is tender.

5 When the vermicelli is cooked, reduce the heat and stir in the chicken pieces and the egg and saffron mixture. Cook the soup over a very low heat for 1–2 minutes, stirring all the time. Serve immediately with Moroccan bread.

Fish with Spinach & Lime

Use fresh spinach for this dish, both for flavour and texture.

Serves 4

INGREDIENTS
675 g/1½ lb white fish, such as
   haddock, cod, sea bass or monkfish
sunflower oil, for frying
500 g/1¼ lb potatoes, sliced
1 onion, chopped
1–2 garlic cloves, crushed
5 tomatoes, peeled and chopped
375 g/13 oz fresh spinach, chopped
lime wedges, to garnish

FOR THE *CHARMOULA*
6 spring onions, chopped
10 ml/2 tsp fresh thyme
60 ml/4 tbsp chopped fresh
   flat leaf parsley
30 ml/2 tbsp chopped fresh coriander
10 ml/2 tsp paprika
generous pinch of cayenne pepper
60 ml/4 tbsp olive oil
grated rind of 1 lime and 60 ml/4 tbsp
   lime juice
salt

1 Cut the fish into large pieces, removing and discarding any skin and bones, and place the pieces in a large shallow dish.

2 Blend together the ingredients for the *charmoula* and season well with salt. Pour over the fish, stir to mix and leave in a cool place, covered with clear film, for 2–4 hours.

3 Heat about 5 mm/¼ in oil in a large, heavy pan, add the slices of potato and fry until they are cooked through and golden. Drain on kitchen paper.

4 Pour off all but 15 ml/1 tbsp of the oil and add the onion, garlic and tomatoes. Cook over a gentle heat for 5–6 minutes, stirring occasionally, until the onion is soft. Place the cooked potato slices on top of the onion, garlic and tomatoes and then pile the chopped spinach into the pan.

5 Place the pieces of fish on top of the spinach and pour over the prepared marinade. Cover tightly and steam for 15–18 minutes, or until the fish and spinach are cooked.

6 After about 8 minutes, carefully stir so that the fish is evenly distributed throughout the dish. Serve garnished with lime wedges.

Monkfish with Tomatoes & Olives

This makes a really delicious lunch or light supper dish. Alternatively, serve as a starter for 6 to 8 people.

Serves 4

INGREDIENTS

675 g/1½ lb monkfish
30 ml/2 tbsp plain flour
5 ml/1 tsp ground coriander
2.5 ml/½ tsp ground turmeric
25 g/1 oz/2 tbsp butter
8 tomatoes, peeled and chopped
2 garlic cloves, finely chopped
15–30 ml/1–2 tbsp olive oil
40 g/1½ oz/5 tbsp pine nuts, toasted
small pieces of preserved lemon
12 black olives, pitted
salt and freshly ground
    black pepper
whole slices of preserved lemon and
    chopped fresh parsley, to garnish

1 Cut the fish into bite-size chunks. Blend together the flour, coriander, turmeric and seasoning. Dust the fish with the seasoned flour and set aside.

2 Melt the butter in a medium non-stick frying pan and fry the chopped tomatoes and garlic over a gentle heat for 6–8 minutes, until the tomatoes have become very thick.

3 Push the tomatoes to the edge of the pan, moisten the pan with a little olive oil and fry the fish in a single layer for 3–5 minutes over a moderate heat, turning frequently. You may have to do this in batches, so as the first batch of fish cooks, place it on top of the tomatoes at the edge of the pan and fry the remaining fish, adding more oil as necessary.

4 When the fish is cooked, add the toasted pine nuts and stir, scraping the base of the pan in the process to remove the glazed tomatoes. The sauce should be thick and slightly charred in places.

5 Rinse the small pieces of preserved lemon in plenty of cold water, remove and discard the pulp and cut the peel into strips.

6 Stir the preserved lemon strips into the tomato sauce with the olives, adjust the seasoning and serve, garnished with whole slices of preserved lemon and fresh parsley.

Sea Bream with Artichokes & Courgettes

The *charmoula* marinade penetrates the fish and gives it a superb flavour.

Serves 4

INGREDIENTS
1 or 2 whole sea bream or sea bass, about
    1.5 kg/3–3½ lb, cleaned and scaled, with
    the head and tail left on
2 onions
2–3 courgettes
4 tomatoes
45 ml/3 tbsp olive oil
5 ml/1 tsp fresh thyme
400 g/14 oz can artichoke hearts
lemon wedges and finely pared rind,
    black olives and fresh coriander leaves,
    to garnish

FOR THE *CHARMOULA*
1 onion, chopped
2 garlic cloves, halved
½ bunch fresh parsley
3–4 fresh coriander sprigs
pinch of paprika
45 ml/3 tbsp olive oil
30 ml/2 tbsp white wine vinegar
15 ml/1 tbsp lemon juice
salt and freshly ground
    black pepper

1 To make the *charmoula* marinade, process all the ingredients together in a food processor or blender with 45 ml/3 tbsp water until the onion is finely chopped and all the ingredients are well combined.

2 Make three or four slashes on both sides of the fish. Place it in a shallow bowl and spread with the prepared *charmoula* marinade, pressing the marinade into both sides of the fish. Set aside for 2–3 hours, turning the fish over occasionally to ensure it is evenly coated.

3 Slice the onions. Top and tail the courgettes and cut them into julienne strips. Peel the tomatoes by first submerging them in boiling water for 30 seconds. Discard the seeds and chop the flesh roughly.

4 Preheat the oven to 220°C/425°F/ Gas 7. Place the prepared onions, courgette strips and tomatoes in a shallow ovenproof dish. Sprinkle with the olive oil, salt and the fresh thyme and roast the vegetables in the oven for 15–20 minutes, until they are softened and slightly charred.

5 Reduce the oven temperature to 180°C/350°F/Gas 4. Add the artichokes to the dish and place the fish, together with the marinade, on top. Pour over 150 ml/¼ pint/⅔ cup water and cover with foil.

6 Bake for 30–35 minutes, until the fish is tender. For the last 5 minutes of cooking, remove the foil to allow the skin to brown lightly. Serve garnished with lemon wedges and strips of rind, olives and coriander.

Monkfish Couscous

If you prefer to steam the couscous, do so over the onions and peppers.

Serves 4

INGREDIENTS
30 ml/2 tbsp olive oil
1 onion, very thinly sliced into rings
25 g/1 oz/3 tbsp raisins
40 g/1½ oz/¼ cup cashew nuts
1 small red pepper, seeded
 and sliced
1 small yellow pepper, seeded
 and sliced
4 tomatoes, peeled, seeded
 and sliced
350 ml/12 fl oz/1½ cups fish stock
675 g/1½ lb monkfish, skinned and
 cut into bite-size chunks
15 ml/1 tbsp chopped fresh parsley
salt and freshly ground black pepper

FOR THE COUSCOUS
275 g/10 oz/1⅔ cups couscous
550 ml/18 fl oz/2½ cups boiling
 vegetable stock or water

1 Heat half the oil and fry about a quarter of the onion rings for 5–6 minutes, until they are a dark golden brown. Transfer to a plate lined with kitchen paper.

2 Add the raisins and stir-fry for 30–60 seconds, until they begin to plump up. Add to the plate with the onion rings. Add the cashew nuts to the pan and stir-fry for 30–60 seconds, until golden. Transfer to the plate.

3 Heat the remaining oil and fry the remaining onion rings until golden, then add the red and yellow pepper slices. Cook for 6–8 minutes, until the peppers are soft. Add the sliced tomatoes and the fish stock and simmer for 10 minutes.

4 Place the couscous in a bowl, pour over the boiling stock or water and stir briefly. Set aside for 10 minutes so that the couscous can absorb the liquid, then fluff it up with a fork. Cover the bowl and keep warm.

5 Add the fish to the peppers and onion, partially cover and simmer for 6–8 minutes, until the fish is tender, stirring gently occasionally. Season to taste.

6 Pour the fish and sauce over the cooked couscous and serve, sprinkled with the chopped fresh parsley and the reserved onion rings, raisins and cashew nuts.

Sea Bass & Fennel Tagine

This is a delicious tagine where the fish is flavoured with *charmoula*, a favourite blend of herbs and spices used especially in fish dishes.

Serves 4

INGREDIENTS

675 g/1½ lb sea bass, monkfish or cod fillets,
    skinned and cut into bite-size chunks
225 g/8 oz raw Mediterranean prawns
30 ml/2 tbsp olive oil
1 onion, chopped
1 fennel bulb, sliced
225 g/8 oz small new potatoes, halved
475 ml/16 fl oz/2 cups fish stock
lemon wedges, to serve (optional)

FOR THE *CHARMOULA*

2 garlic cloves, crushed
20 ml/4 tsp ground cumin
20 ml/4 tsp paprika
pinch of chilli powder or
    cayenne pepper
30 ml/2 tbsp chopped fresh parsley
30 ml/2 tbsp chopped
    fresh coriander
45 ml/3 tbsp white wine vinegar
15 ml/1 tbsp lemon juice

1 To make the *charmoula,* blend the garlic, spices, herbs, vinegar and lemon juice together in a bowl.

2 Place the fish and prawns in two separate shallow dishes, add half the *charmoula* marinade to each dish and stir well to coat evenly. Cover with clear film and set aside in a cool place for 30 minutes–2 hours.

3 Heat the oil in a flameproof casserole and fry the onion for 2 minutes. Add the fennel and cook over gentle heat for 5–6 minutes, until flecked with brown. Add the potatoes and stock and cook for 10–15 minutes, until the potatoes are tender.

4 Add the marinated fish, stir gently and cook for 4 minutes, then add the prawns and all the remaining marinade and cook for a further 5–6 minutes, until the fish is tender and the prawns are pink. Serve with lemon wedges if you wish.

Moroccan Roast Chicken

Flavoured with a tasty Moroccan-style marinade, this chicken is excellent cooked whole, halved or in quarters.

Serves 4–6

INGREDIENTS
1.75 kg/4–4½ lb chicken
2 small shallots
1 garlic clove
1 fresh parsley sprig
1 fresh coriander sprig
5 ml/1 tsp salt
7.5 ml/1½ tsp paprika
pinch of cayenne pepper
5–7.5 ml/1–1½ tsp ground cumin
about 40 g/1½ oz/3 tbsp butter
½–1 lemon (optional)
sprigs of fresh parsley or coriander,
   to garnish

1 Unless cooking it whole, cut the chicken in half or into quarters using poultry shears or a sharp knife.

2 Process the shallots, garlic, herbs, salt and spices in a food processor until finely chopped. Add the butter and process to make a smooth paste.

3 Thoroughly rub the paste over the skin of the chicken and then allow it to stand for 1–2 hours.

4 Preheat the oven to 200°C/400°F/ Gas 6 and put the chicken in a roasting tin. If using, quarter the lemon and place one or two quarters around the chicken pieces (or in the body cavity if the chicken is whole) and squeeze a little juice over the skin.

5 Roast in the oven for 1–1¼ hours (2–2½ hours for a whole bird), until the chicken is cooked through and the meat juices run clear when pierced with the point of a knife. Baste the meat occasionally. If the skin starts to brown too quickly, cover the chicken loosely with foil.

6 Allow the chicken to stand, covered, for 5–10 minutes before carving, then serve garnished with parsley or coriander.

Chicken with Preserved Lemon & Olives

Preserved lemon is essential for this famous Moroccan dish as fresh lemon simply doesn't have the required mellow flavour.

Serves 4

INGREDIENTS
30 ml/2 tbsp olive oil
1 Spanish onion, chopped
3 garlic cloves, crushed
1 cm/½ in fresh root ginger, grated, or
    2.5 ml/½ tsp ground ginger
2.5–5 ml/½–1 tsp ground cinnamon
pinch of saffron
4 chicken quarters, preferably breasts,
    halved if liked
750 ml/1¼ pints/3 cups chicken stock
30 ml/2 tbsp chopped fresh coriander
30 ml/2 tbsp chopped fresh parsley
1 preserved lemon
115 g/4 oz/⅔ cup Moroccan tan olives
salt and freshly ground black pepper
lemon wedges and fresh coriander sprigs,
    to garnish

1 Heat the oil in a large, flameproof casserole and fry the onion for 6–8 minutes over moderate heat, until lightly golden, stirring occasionally.

2 Meanwhile, blend the garlic with the ginger, cinnamon, saffron and a little salt and pepper. Stir into the pan and fry for 1 minute. Add the chicken pieces, in batches if necessary, and fry over a moderate heat for 2–3 minutes, until lightly browned.

3 Add the chicken stock, fresh coriander and parsley, bring the liquid to the boil, then cover and leave to simmer very gently for 45 minutes, until the chicken is tender.

4 Rinse the preserved lemon under cold water, discard the flesh and cut the peel into small pieces. Stir the peel, along with the olives, into the pan containing the chicken and allow to simmer for a further 15 minutes, until the chicken is very tender.

5 Transfer the chicken pieces to a plate and keep warm. Bring the sauce to the boil and cook for 3–4 minutes, until it has reduced and is fairly thick. Pour the sauce over the chicken and serve immediately, garnished with lemon wedges and coriander sprigs.

Chicken & Apricot Filo Pie

This light but satisfying pie combines minced chicken with apricots, bulgur wheat, nuts, herbs and spices.

Serves 6

INGREDIENTS
75 g/3 oz/½ cup bulgur wheat
75 g/3 oz/6 tbsp butter
1 onion, chopped
450 g/1 lb minced chicken
50 g/2 oz/¼ cup ready-to-eat dried
   apricots, finely chopped
25 g/1 oz/¼ cup blanched
   almonds, chopped
5 ml/1 tsp ground cinnamon
2.5 ml/½ tsp ground allspice
50 ml/2 fl oz/¼ cup Greek yogurt
15 ml/1 tbsp snipped fresh chives
30 ml/2 tbsp chopped fresh parsley
6 large sheets filo pastry
salt and freshly ground
   black pepper
fresh chives, to garnish

1 Preheat the oven to 200°C/400°F/Gas 6. Put the bulgur wheat in a bowl with 120 ml/4 fl oz/½ cup boiling water and soak for 5–10 minutes, until the water is absorbed.

2 Heat 25 g/1 oz/2 tbsp of the butter in a pan and gently fry the onion and chicken until pale golden. Stir in the apricots, almonds and bulgur wheat and cook for a further 2 minutes. Remove from the heat and stir in the spices, yogurt and chopped herbs. Season to taste.

3 Melt the remaining butter. Cut the filo pastry into 25 cm/10 in rounds.

4 Line a 23 cm/9 in loose-based flan tin with three of the pastry rounds, brushing each one with butter as you layer them.

5 Spoon the chicken mixture on to the pastry layer and cover with three more pastry rounds, brushed with melted butter as before.

6 Crumple the remaining pastry rounds and place them on top of the pie, then brush over any remaining melted butter.

7 Bake the pie for about 30 minutes, until the pastry is golden brown and crisp. Serve hot or cold, garnished with fresh chives.

COOK'S TIP: To prevent the filo pastry drying out keep any unused sheets covered with a damp dish towel.

Stuffed Kibbeh

This is a tasty North African speciality of minced meat and bulgur wheat. The patties are sometimes stuffed with extra meat and deep fried.

Serves 4–6

INGREDIENTS
225 g/8 oz/1⅓ cups bulgur wheat
1 red chilli, seeded and roughly chopped
1 onion, roughly chopped
450 g/1 lb lean minced lamb
oil, for deep frying
salt and freshly ground black pepper
avocado slices and coriander sprigs,
    to serve

FOR THE STUFFING
1 onion, finely chopped
50 g/2 oz/6 tbsp pine nuts
30 ml/2 tbsp olive oil
7.5 ml/1½ tsp ground allspice
60 ml/4 tbsp chopped
    fresh coriander

1 Soak the bulgur wheat in cold water for 15 minutes. Drain well, then process in a blender or food processor with the chilli, onion, half the meat and plenty of seasoning.

2 To make the stuffing, fry the onion and pine nuts in the oil for 5 minutes. Add the allspice and remaining minced meat and fry gently, stirring, until browned. Add the coriander and a little seasoning.

3 Turn the bulgur wheat mixture out on to a work surface and shape into a cake. Cut into 12 wedges.

4 Flatten one piece in your hand and spoon a little stuffing into the centre. Bring the edges up to enclose it. Form into an egg-shape, ensuring that the filling is encased. Make the others in the same way.

5 Heat the oil to a depth of 5 cm/ 2 in in a large pan until a few *kibbeh* crumbs sizzle on the surface. Fry half the *kibbeh* for about 5 minutes, until golden. Drain and keep hot while cooking the remainder. Serve with avocado slices and coriander sprigs.

Lamb & Pumpkin Couscous

A traditional recipe, with echoes of the very early vegetable couscous dishes made by the Berbers.

Serves 4–6

INGREDIENTS
75 g/3 oz/½ cup chick-peas,
   soaked overnight
675 g/1½ lb lean lamb, cut into
   bite-size pieces
2 Spanish onions, sliced
pinch of saffron
1.5 ml/¼ tsp ground ginger
2.5 ml/½ tsp ground turmeric
5 ml/1 tsp freshly ground black pepper
450 g/1 lb carrots, cut into 6 cm/2½ in pieces
675 g/1½ lb pumpkin, peeled, seeded and cut
   into 2.5 cm/1 in cubes
75 g/3 oz/⅔ cup raisins
400 g/14 oz/2⅓ cups couscous
salt
fresh parsley, to garnish

1 Drain the chick-peas and cook for 1–1½ hours in boiling water, until tender. Place in cold water and remove the skins with your fingers. Discard the skins and drain.

2 Place the lamb, onions, saffron, ginger, turmeric, pepper, salt and 1.2 litres/2 pints/5 cups water in a couscousier or large saucepan. Slowly bring to the boil, then cover and simmer for about 1 hour, until the meat is tender.

3 Stir the carrots, pumpkin and raisins into the meat mixture, cover and simmer for a further 30–35 minutes, until the vegetables and meat are completely tender.

4 Prepare the couscous according to the instructions on the packet. Spoon on to a warmed serving plate, making a well in the centre.

5 Spoon the stew and gravy into the centre of the couscous, arranging some carrots down the sides, or alternatively stir the stew into the couscous. Pour extra gravy into a jug. Garnish with parsley and serve.

Moroccan Stuffed Leg of Lamb

Moroccans always serve meat very well cooked. If you prefer lamb slightly pink, reduce the cooking time a little.

Serves 6

INGREDIENTS
1.5 kg/3–3½ lb leg of lamb, boned
2 garlic cloves, crushed
40 g/1½ oz/3 tbsp butter
175 ml/6 fl oz/¾ cup chicken stock
15 ml/1 tbsp cornflour
15 ml/1 tbsp apricot jam
salt and freshly ground black pepper

FOR THE STUFFING
1 green chilli, seeded
2 shallots
1 garlic clove
1 bunch fresh coriander
sprig of fresh parsley
25 g/1 oz/2 tbsp butter
10 ml/2 tsp ground cumin
2.5 ml/½ tsp ground cinnamon
150 g/5 oz/¾ cup cooked
   long grain rice
30 ml/2 tbsp pine nuts

1 Preheat the oven to 200°C/400°F/ Gas 6. To make the stuffing, finely chop the chilli, shallots, garlic and herbs in a food processor.

2 Fry the shallot, chilli and herb mixture gently in the butter for 2–3 minutes to soften the shallots. Stir in the spices.

3 Place the cooked rice in a bowl, add the pine nuts and then stir in the rest of the stuffing ingredients from the pan. Season well with salt and freshly ground black pepper.

4 Season the meat on both sides and rub the outside with the crushed garlic and butter. Place the meat, skin side down, on a work surface and spread the stuffing evenly over it. Roll the meat around the stuffing, secure the roll with a skewer and tie with cooking string at even intervals along the roll.

5 Place the meat in a roasting tin and cook in the oven for 20 minutes, then reduce the heat to 180°C/350°F/ Gas 4 and continue to roast for a further 1½–2 hours. Baste the meat during the cooking process. Remove the meat from the roasting tin.

6 To make the sauce, pour away the excess fat from the roasting tin and add the stock. Heat gently, stirring all the time, to deglaze the tin. Blend the cornflour with 30 ml/2 tbsp water and add to the roasting tin with the apricot jam. Gradually bring to the boil, stirring all the time. Strain the thickened sauce into a serving jug and serve with the stuffed leg of lamb.

43

Beef Tagine with Sweet Potatoes

This warming dish is eaten during the winter in Morocco, where, especially in the mountains, the weather can be surprisingly cold.

Serves 4

INGREDIENTS
675–900 g/1½–2 lb braising or stewing beef
30 ml/2 tbsp sunflower oil
good pinch of ground turmeric
1 large onion, chopped
1 red or green chilli, seeded and chopped
7.5 ml/1½ tsp paprika
good pinch of cayenne pepper
2.5 ml/½ tsp ground cumin
450 g/1 lb sweet potatoes
15 ml/1 tbsp chopped fresh parsley
15 ml/1 tbsp chopped fresh coriander
15 g/½ oz/1 tbsp butter
salt and freshly ground black pepper

1 Cut the meat into 2 cm/¾ in cubes. Heat the oil in a flameproof casserole and fry the meat with the turmeric and seasoning over a medium heat for 3–4 minutes, until evenly brown, stirring frequently.

2 Cover the casserole tightly with a lid or foil and cook the meat for 15 minutes over a fairly gentle heat, without uncovering. Preheat the oven to 180°C/350°F/Gas 4.

3 Add the chopped onion and chilli, along with the paprika, cayenne pepper and cumin to the casserole together with just enough water to cover the meat. Cover the casserole tightly and cook in the oven for 1–1½ hours, until the meat is very tender, adding a little extra water as necessary to keep the consistency of the stew fairly moist.

4 Meanwhile, peel the sweet potatoes and slice them straight into a bowl of salted water. Transfer to a pan along with the water, bring to the boil and simmer for 2–3 minutes, until just tender. Drain well.

5 Stir the fresh parsley and coriander into the meat mixture, arrange the sweet potato slices over the top and dot with the butter. Cover the casserole and cook in the oven for a further 10 minutes, or until the potatoes feel very tender.

6 Increase the oven temperature to 200°C/400°F/Gas 6. Remove the lid of the casserole and allow to cook for a further 5–10 minutes, until the layer of sweet potatoes is golden. Serve the tagine at once, whilst it is still piping hot.

Broad Beans with Herbs

Peeling the broad beans is time-consuming but worthwhile.

Serves 4

INGREDIENTS
350 g/12 oz frozen broad beans
15 g/½ oz/1 tbsp butter
4–5 spring onions, sliced
15 ml/1 tbsp chopped fresh coriander
5 ml/1 tsp chopped fresh mint
2.5–5 ml/½–1 tsp ground cumin
10 ml/2 tsp olive oil
salt

1 Simmer the broad beans in water for 3–4 minutes until tender. Drain and, when cool enough to handle, peel away the outer skin, so you are left with the bright green seed.

2 Melt the butter in a small pan and gently fry the onions for 2–3 minutes. Add the beans and then stir in the herbs, cumin and a pinch of salt. Stir in the olive oil and serve immediately.

Courgettes with Spices

This is a delicious way of cooking courgettes, especially young ones.

Serves 4

INGREDIENTS
500 g/1¼ lb courgettes
lemon juice and chopped fresh coriander
  and parsley, to serve

FOR THE SPICY *CHARMOULA*
1 onion
1–2 garlic cloves, crushed
¼ red or green chilli, seeded and sliced
2.5 ml/½ tsp paprika
2.5 ml/½ tsp ground cumin
45 ml/3 tbsp olive oil
salt and freshly ground
  black pepper

1 Preheat the oven to 180°C/350°F/ Gas 4. Cut the courgettes lengthways, and place in a shallow, ovenproof dish.

2 Finely chop the onion and blend with the other *charmoula* ingredients and 60 ml/4 tbsp water. Pour over the courgettes. Cover with foil and bake for about 15 minutes. Baste the courgettes and cook, uncovered, for 5–10 minutes more, until tender. Sprinkle with lemon juice and herbs and serve.

Right: Broad Beans with Herbs (top);
Courgettes with Spices

Spinach with Beans, Raisins & Pine Nuts

This dish is traditionally made with chick-peas, but can be made with haricot beans as here. Use either dried or canned beans.

Serves 4

INGREDIENTS
115 g/4 oz/scant ¾ cup haricot beans,
　soaked overnight, or 400 g/14 oz
　can, drained
60 ml/4 tbsp olive oil
1 thick slice white bread
1 onion, chopped
3–4 tomatoes, peeled, seeded
　and chopped
2.5 ml/½ tsp ground cumin
5 ml/1 tsp paprika
450 g/1 lb spinach
1 garlic clove, halved
25 g/1 oz/3 tbsp raisins
25 g/1 oz/3 tbsp pine nuts, toasted
salt and freshly ground
　black pepper
Moroccan bread, to serve

1 If using soaked, dried beans, drain and cook them in fresh boiling water for about 1 hour, until tender. Drain. Heat 30 ml/2 tbsp of the oil in a frying pan and fry the bread until golden. Transfer to a plate.

2 Fry the onion in a further 15 ml/ 1 tbsp of the oil over a gentle heat until soft but not brown, then add the tomatoes and cumin and continue cooking gently.

3 Heat the remaining olive oil in a large pan, stir in the paprika and then add the spinach and 45 ml/3 tbsp water. Cover the pan and cook for a few minutes, until the spinach has just wilted.

4 Add the onion and tomato mixture to the spinach and stir in the beans, then season with salt and freshly ground black pepper.

5 Place the garlic and fried bread in a food processor and blend until smooth. Stir into the spinach and bean mixture, together with the raisins. Add 175 ml/6 fl oz/¾ cup water, cover and simmer gently for 20–30 minutes, adding more water if necessary.

6 Scatter the spinach with toasted pine nuts and serve, accompanied by Moroccan bread.

Chick-pea Tagine

A simple-to-make vegetable dish, bursting with the flavours of Morocco.

Serves 4–6

INGREDIENTS
150 g/5 oz/¾ cup chick-peas,
    soaked overnight, or 2 x 400 g/
    14 oz cans, drained
30 ml/2 tbsp sunflower oil
1 large onion, chopped
1 garlic clove, crushed (optional)
400 g/14 oz can chopped tomatoes
5 ml/1 tsp ground cumin
350 ml/12 fl oz/1½ cups
    vegetable stock
¼ preserved lemon
30 ml/2 tbsp chopped
    fresh coriander
Moroccan bread, to serve

1 If using dried chick-peas, cook in boiling water for 1–1½ hours, until they are tender. Drain. Skin the chick-peas by placing them in a bowl of cold water and rubbing them between your fingers – the skins will rise to the surface. Discard the skins and drain the chick-peas.

2 Heat the oil in a saucepan or flameproof casserole and fry the onion and the crushed garlic, if using, for 8–10 minutes, until golden.

3 Stir in the chick-peas, tomatoes, cumin and stock. Simmer, uncovered, for 30–40 minutes, until the chick-peas are very soft and most of the liquid has evaporated.

4 Rinse the preserved lemon and cut away the flesh and pith. Cut the peel into slivers and stir into the chick-peas along with the coriander. Serve immediately with Moroccan bread.

Schlada

This is the Moroccan cousin of gazpacho – indeed the word *gazpacho* is Arabic in origin, meaning soaked bread.

Serves 4

INGREDIENTS
3 green peppers
4 large tomatoes
2 garlic cloves, finely chopped
30 ml/2 tbsp olive oil
30 ml/2 tbsp lemon juice
good pinch of paprika
pinch of ground cumin
¼ preserved lemon
salt and freshly ground black pepper
fresh coriander and flat leaf parsley,
    to garnish

1 Place the green peppers under a preheated grill. When the skins are soft and blackened, place the peppers in a plastic bag and tie the ends of the bag together. Leave the skins for about 10 minutes, until the peppers are cool enough to handle, then remove them from the bag and carefully peel away the charred skins.

2 Cut the peppers into small pieces, discarding the seeds and core, and place in a serving dish.

3 Peel the tomatoes by placing in boiling water for 1 minute, then plunging into cold water. Peel off the skins, then quarter the tomatoes, discarding the core and seeds. Chop roughly and add to the peppers. Scatter the chopped garlic on top and chill for 1 hour.

4 Blend together the olive oil, lemon juice, paprika and cumin and pour over the peppers and tomatoes. Season with salt and pepper.

5 Rinse the preserved lemon in plenty of cold water and remove the flesh and pith. Cut the lemon peel into fine slivers and sprinkle over the peppers and tomatoes. Garnish the salad with fresh coriander and flat leaf parsley and serve immediately.

Date, Orange & Carrot Salad

This is a colourful and unusual salad made with exotic ingredients.

Serves 4

INGREDIENTS
1 Little Gem lettuce
2 carrots, finely grated
2 oranges
115 g/4 oz fresh dates, stoned and cut
      lengthways into eighths
25 g/1 oz/¼ cup toasted whole
      almonds, chopped
30 ml/2 tbsp lemon juice
5 ml/1 tsp caster sugar
1.5 ml/¼ tsp salt
15 ml/1 tbsp orange flower water

1 Arrange the lettuce leaves in a salad bowl or on individual plates. Place the grated carrot in a mound on top of the leaves.

2 Peel and segment the oranges and arrange them around the carrot. Pile the date pieces on top, then sprinkle with the almonds.

3 Mix together the lemon juice, sugar, salt and orange flower water and sprinkle over the salad ingredients. Serve the salad chilled.

Couscous Salad

This is a spicy variation on tabbouleh, traditionally made with bulgur wheat.

Serves 4

INGREDIENTS

45 ml/3 tbsp olive oil
5 spring onions, chopped
1 garlic clove, crushed
5 ml/1 tsp ground cumin
350 ml/12 fl oz/1½ cups vegetable stock
175 g/6 oz/1 cup couscous
2 tomatoes, peeled and chopped
60 ml/4 tbsp chopped fresh parsley
60 ml/4 tbsp chopped fresh mint
1 green chilli, seeded and
    finely chopped
30 ml/2 tbsp lemon juice
salt and freshly ground black pepper
toasted pine nuts and grated lemon rind,
    to garnish
crisp lettuce leaves, to serve

1 Heat the olive oil, add the spring onions, garlic and cumin and cook for 1 minute. Add the vegetable stock and bring to the boil.

2 Remove the pan from the heat, stir in the couscous, cover and leave to stand for 10 minutes, until all the liquid has been absorbed.

3 Tip the couscous into a bowl. Stir in the tomatoes, herbs, chilli, lemon juice, salt and pepper. If possible, leave to stand for up to an hour.

4 To serve, line a bowl with lettuce leaves and spoon the couscous salad into the centre. Garnish with pine nuts and lemon rind and serve.

Moroccan Serpent Cake

This is perhaps the most famous of all Moroccan pastries, filled with lightly fragrant almond paste.

Serves 8

INGREDIENTS
8 sheets filo pastry
50 g/2 oz/¼ cup butter, melted
1 egg, beaten
5 ml/1 tsp ground cinnamon
icing sugar, for dusting

FOR THE ALMOND PASTE
about 50 g/2 oz/¼ cup
    butter, melted
225 g/8 oz/2 cups ground almonds
2.5 ml/½ tsp almond essence
50 g/2 oz/½ cup icing sugar
1 egg yolk, beaten
15 ml/1 tbsp rose water or orange flower
    water (optional)

1 To make the almond paste, blend the butter with the ground almonds and almond essence. Add the icing sugar, egg yolk and rose or orange flower water, if using. Mix well and knead until pliable. Chill the paste for about 10 minutes.

2 Break the piece of almond paste into 10 even-size balls and roll into 10 cm/4 in "sausages". Chill again.

3 Preheat the oven to 180°C/350°F/ Gas 4. Place two sheets of filo pastry overlapping to form an 18 x 56 cm/ 7 x 22 in rectangle. Brush the overlapping pastry to secure and then brush all over with butter. Cover with another two sheets and brush again.

4 Place five "sausages" of almond paste along the long edge of the filo and roll up tightly, tucking in the ends. Repeat with the remaining filo and almond paste. Join the two lengths and coil to make a "snake". Place on a buttered baking sheet.

5 Beat together the egg and half the cinnamon. Brush over the snake and bake for 20–25 minutes, until golden. Invert and bake for 5–10 minutes more. Serve warm, dusted with icing sugar and the remaining cinnamon.

Moroccan Rice Pudding

A simple and delicious alternative to traditional rice pudding.

Serves 6

INGREDIENTS
25 g/1 oz/¼ cup blanched
  almonds, chopped
450 g/1 lb/2¼ cups pudding rice
25 g/1 oz/¼ cup icing sugar, plus extra for
  serving (optional)
7.5 cm/3 in cinnamon stick
50 g/2 oz/¼ cup butter, plus extra, to serve
1.5 ml/¼ tsp almond essence
175 ml/6 fl oz/¾ cup milk mixed
  with 175 ml/6 fl oz/¾ cup
  condensed milk
30 ml/2 tbsp orange flower water
pinch of salt
toasted flaked almonds and ground
  cinnamon, to decorate

1 Process the almonds in a food processor with 60 ml/4 tbsp very hot water. Push through a sieve into a bowl. Add a further 60 ml/4 tbsp very hot water and process again. Push through the sieve into a pan.

2 Add 300 ml/½ pint/1¼ cups water and bring to the boil. Add the rice, sugar, cinnamon stick, butter, salt, almond essence and half the milk.

3 Simmer, covered, for 30 minutes. Stir in the remaining milk, until thick. Add the orange flower water, plus extra sugar if liked. To serve, dot with the remaining butter and sprinkle with almonds and cinnamon.

Stuffed Apricots

Almonds have a delightful affinity with apricots.

Serves 6

INGREDIENTS
75 g/3 oz/scant ½ cup caster sugar
30 ml/2 tbsp lemon juice
115 g/4 oz/1 cup ground almonds
50 g/2 oz/½ cup icing sugar or caster sugar
a little orange flower water (optional)
25 g/1 oz/2 tbsp melted butter
2.5 ml/½ tsp almond essence
900 g/2 lb fresh apricots
fresh mint sprigs, to decorate

1 Preheat the oven to 180°C/350°F/ Gas 4. Bring the sugar, lemon juice and 300 ml/½ pint/1¼ cups water to the boil and simmer for 5–10 minutes.

2 In a bowl, blend together the ground almonds, icing or caster sugar, orange flower water, if using, melted butter and almond essence to form a smooth paste.

3 Slit each apricot and ease out the stone. Stuff each fruit with a small piece of the almond paste.

4 Put the stuffed apricots in a shallow ovenproof dish and pour over the sugar syrup. Cover the dish with foil and bake the stuffed apricots for 25–30 minutes. Serve with a little of the syrup, if liked, and decorated with sprigs of fresh mint.

Gazelles' Horns

Kaab el Ghzal is one of Morocco's favourite and best-known pastries.

Makes about 16

INGREDIENTS
200 g/7 oz/1¾ cups plain flour
25 g/1 oz/2 tbsp melted butter
about 30 ml/2 tbsp orange flower water
    or water
1 large egg yolk, beaten
pinch of salt
icing sugar, to serve

FOR THE ALMOND PASTE
200 g/7 oz/scant 2 cups
    ground almonds
115 g/4 oz/1 cup icing sugar or
    caster sugar
30 ml/2 tbsp orange flower water
25 g/1 oz/2 tbsp melted butter
2 egg yolks, beaten
2.5 ml/½ tsp ground cinnamon

1 To make the almond paste, mix together all the ingredients until smoothly blended.

2 Mix the flour and salt, then stir in the butter, orange flower water or water and about three-quarters of the egg yolk. Stir in a little cold water, to make a fairly soft dough.

3 Knead the dough for about 10 minutes, until it is smooth and elastic, then roll it out as thinly as possible. Cut the dough into long strips about 7.5 cm/3 in wide.

4 Preheat the oven to 180°C/350°F/Gas 4. Roll small pieces of the almond paste between your hands into thin "sausages" about 7.5 cm/3 in long with tapering ends.

5 Place these in a line along one side of the strips of pastry, leaving a gap of about 3 cm/1¼ in between them. Dampen the pastry edges with water, then fold the other half of the strip over the filling and press the edges together firmly.

6 Using a pastry wheel, cut around each "sausage" (as you would with ravioli) to make a crescent shape. Make sure that the edges are firmly pinched together.

7 Prick the crescent shapes with a fork and place them on a buttered baking tray. Brush with the remaining egg yolk and bake for 12–16 minutes, until lightly coloured. Cool and then dust with icing sugar.

Moroccan Bread

Warm this bread in the oven and cut it into thick slices to serve with any classic Moroccan savoury dish.

Makes 2 loaves

INGREDIENTS
275 g/10 oz/2½ cups strong
   white flour
175 g/6 oz/1½ cups wholemeal flour
10 ml/2 tsp salt
about 250 ml/8 fl oz/1 cup warm milk and
   water mixed
10 ml/2 tsp sesame seeds

FOR THE YEAST STARTER
150 ml/¼ pint/⅔ cup warm milk and
   water mixed
5 ml/1 tsp sugar
10 ml/2 tsp dried yeast

1 To prepare the yeast starter, combine the warm milk and water mixture and the sugar in a small bowl or jug, then sprinkle in the dried yeast. Stir and set aside in a warm place for about 10 minutes, until frothy.

2 Mix together the two flours and salt. Add the yeast mixture and enough of the warm milk and water to make a fairly soft dough. Knead for 10–12 minutes, until firm and elastic.

3 Break the dough into two and form into flattened ball shapes. Place on floured baking trays and press into rounds about 13–15 cm/5–6 in across.

4 Cover with a clean, damp cloth and set aside for 1–1½ hours in a warm place, until risen. The dough is ready to bake when it springs back if gently pressed with a finger.

5 Preheat the oven to 200°C/400°F/ Gas 6. Sprinkle the loaves with sesame seeds and bake for 12 minutes. Reduce the temperature to 150°C/300°F/ Gas 2 and bake for 20–30 minutes more, until the loaves are golden and sound hollow if tapped.

Index

This edition is published by Hermes House

© Anness Publishing Limited 1999, updated 2001, 2002.

Hermes House is an imprint of Anness Publishing Limited,
Hermes House, 88–89 Blackfriars Road, London SE1 8HA

Publisher: Joanna Lorenz
Editor: Valerie Ferguson
Series Designer: Bobbie Colgate Stone
Designer: Andrew Heath
Production Controller: Joanna King

Recipes contributed by: Joanna Farrow,
Rebekah Hassan, Lesley Mackley.

Photography: William Adams-Lingwood,
Michelle Garrett.

3 5 7 9 10 8 6 4

Notes:
For all recipes, quantities are given in both metric and imperial measures and, where appropriate, measures are also given in standard cups and spoons. Follow one set, but not a mixture, because they are not interchangeable.

Standard spoon and cup measures are level.

1 tsp = 5 ml   1 tbsp =15 ml   1 cup = 250 ml/8 fl oz

Australian standard tablespoons are 20 ml. Australian readers should use 3 tsp in place of 1 tbsp for measuring small quantities of gelatine, cornflour, salt, etc.

Medium eggs are used unless otherwise stated.

Printed in China